Help with reading aloud

- If you have time, try reading the book by yourself first. Practise reading it out loud.
- You may not know all the words, but don't worry. If you are not sure how to say a word, split it up into parts and sound it out, e.g. comfortable would be com-for-ta-ble.
- If you are not sure what a word means, look at the pictures to see if there are any clues that may help.
- Some of the names are made up for the Amazing Travelling Space Circus. Look at the pages at the front of the book which show all the characters.

Next step

If you would like to find more help with reading, there are BBC RaW book groups all round the country. Call 0800 0150 950 to find your nearest RaW centre and to get some free advice on what to do next. Or visit our website (bbc.co.uk/raw) and enter your postcode to find your nearest RaW centre.

Published by the BBC
201 Wood Lane
London W12 7TS

© BBC 2007
All rights reserved.
Reproduction in whole or in part
prohibited without permission.

ISBN 978-1-86000-236-6

Written by Heather Morris

Illustrated by Peter Lawson

Characters created by
Firedog Design

Designed by Starfish Design,
Editorial and Project
Management Ltd

Printed in Great Britain by ESP
Colour Ltd

Printed on paper manufactured
from sustainable forests

In this book you will meet ...

Guv
the Ringmaster
Always busy running the circus – he's loved by everyone. He's quite old and needs his aerial soapbox to get around.

Gobi
the Circus Roustabout
He's the circus handyman. Gobi's only happy when inventing, fixing or playing with machines. He sulks if people don't pay attention to him.

Mrs. Spectacles
The Ringmaster's wife, she runs the circus. She's a clever old woman who plans everything and looks after everyone.

Lokankee
the Great Escape Artist
He can slip in and out of the smallest spaces. He can escape from anywhere which is why he is called lok-an-kee (lock and key).

Mr. Scatterbrain
the Clown
He loves to entertain people and make them laugh. He rides a jet-powered unicorn.

Magu
the Marvellous Magician
Magu is always showing off his magic tricks. He thinks everyone wants to be like him but they really find him a bit annoying.

The circus finds a new star

How to use this book

Enjoy reading this book together with a child. You don't have to read it all in one go. Find a relaxed time and somewhere you can be comfortable. If you have time, you could read it by yourself first. If you just look at the pictures and read the speech bubbles these will tell you the main events in the story.

When you are sharing the book, you could read the main story text. Help the child to join in.

- Ask them to read the text in the speech bubbles if they are starting to read.
- Encourage them to talk about details in the pictures.
- Guess what might happen next before you turn the page.
- Talk about the questions at the end of the page.

Above all, just enjoy sharing the story together.

Tiny
the Strongoid

A tiny girl who loves to play. She's pretty but so strong she often breaks things. The earth shakes when she skips.

Baked Bean
the Embarrassed Dragon

A shy green dragon who is very embarrassed because he can't fly or breathe fire like other dragons.

Monstro
the Master of Disguise

He wants to join the circus but all the shapes he creates are just too horrible. But he discovers another talent instead.

The Fabulous Fireflies

They create magic glowing shapes when they fly. The faster they flap their wings, the more brightly they glow.

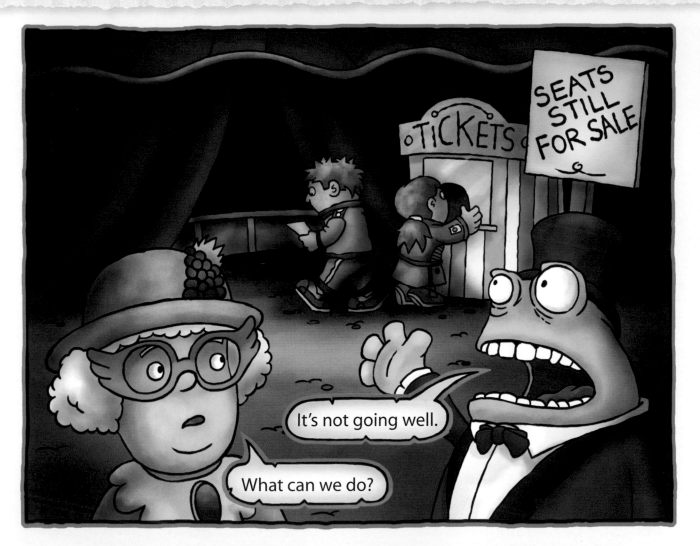

Guv and Mrs. Spectacles are worried. They have been running the Amazing Travelling Space Circus all over the galaxy for twenty years. It's always been very popular, but suddenly people aren't coming. Even the food isn't selling any more. Things are getting serious.

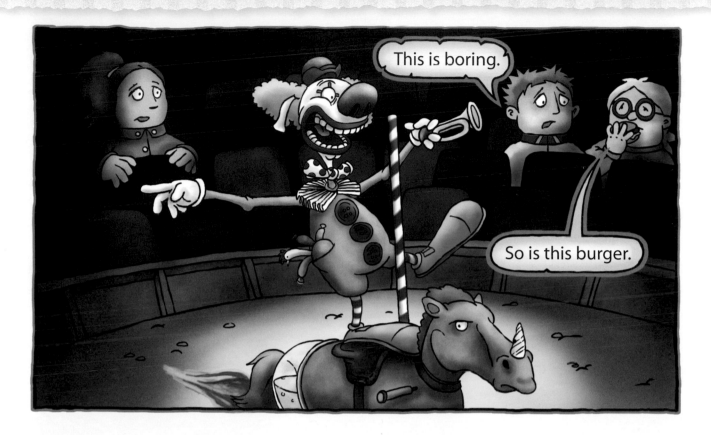

Mr. Scatterbrain is having a hard time. The crowd just doesn't find him funny any more. The harder he tries, the less it works. He blows his horn. There is silence. He makes his eyes flash and his hat whirl round. Nobody laughs. He squirts water from his bow tie. The people he hits get cross.

Mr. Scatterbrain panics and stands up on his jet-powered unicorn. He balances shakily on one leg. A few people clap. Mr. Scatterbrain tries to take a bow and falls flat on his face on the ring. At last the audience laughs.

Guv and Mrs. Spectacles discuss what to do. 'We need to find some new acts,' says Guv. 'People are bored with what we have been doing. We'll hold a competition to find new talent.'

'We also need new tricks for our old acts,' says Mrs. Spectacles. 'I'm sure they can think up some.'

'Well, I'm not falling off my unicorn again,' moans Mr. Scatterbrain. 'My nose is still so sore I don't need my false red one.'

'We'll give everyone a month and then we'll hold auditions for all the acts,' Guv decides.

'And we must do something about the food,' Mrs. Spectacles adds.

It is the day of the auditions. Everyone in the circus has been working hard. Even Mr. Scatterbrain has been practising his act. Now he can balance on his unicorn and then fall off without landing on his nose! As well as the usual acts there are some new ones who have come to try their luck. It is going to be a long day.

The first to go are Lokankee and Magu, the Marvellous Magician. Lokankee can escape from any space. He has challenged Magu to create new places for him to escape from. So far he has managed to wriggle out of them all.

First Magu produces a huge chest with iron chains and a giant padlock. He locks Lokankee inside the chest. But Lokankee just slides out through the keyhole!

Then Magu puts him into a bag tied at both ends. He puts the bag inside a sack. Then he hangs the sack up with a long piece of rope. The sack heaves and bulges. Finally Lokankee wriggles out through the top looking as thin as a piece of rope himself!

For his last trick Magu blows a huge bubble round Lokankee and he floats away up into the Big Top. Inside the bubble, Lokankee takes a deep breath and blows and blows until the bubble bursts. He slides down the tent pole into the ring. Everyone claps loudly.

Can you think of some places for Lokankee to escape from?

Tiny the Strongoid has always been popular in the circus. She looks so small but is so strong. She can lift huge weights and break iron bars. She tried and tried but she wasn't able to think of anything new to do.

Then one day she and Baked Bean were playing. Tiny was swinging him round her head and let go of him by accident. Baked Bean suddenly discovered he could fly. Before this he'd never been able to get off the ground. Now he

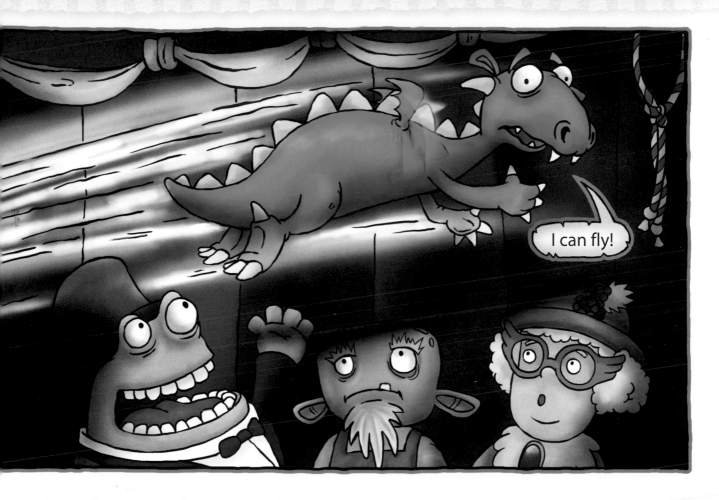

loves flying over the seats in the Big Top.

There is only one thing that Baked Bean is sad about. He still can't breathe fire.

He thinks all real dragons should be able to do this.

But Guv and Mrs. Spectacles are delighted to have a flying dragon. Even Gobi is a bit impressed.

The next act is a new one. He calls himself Monstro the Master of Disguise. When he arrives he looks quite normal – for a Space Circus at least. He strides into the ring and waves a huge purple cape over his head. Monstro disappears and a new shape appears in the ring. It is a bit like an orange jelly that someone has sat on. It is impressive, but not very pretty.

The cape waves again and this time what comes out is just horrible. Big green eyes at the end of long snaky arms wave above a blobby body. Guv stands up to tell him to stop, but before he can speak the cape waves again.

This time everyone gasps. The third shape is truly awful. They all start to shout 'Get off', and Baked Bean bursts into tears. This is one act that isn't going to be in the circus.

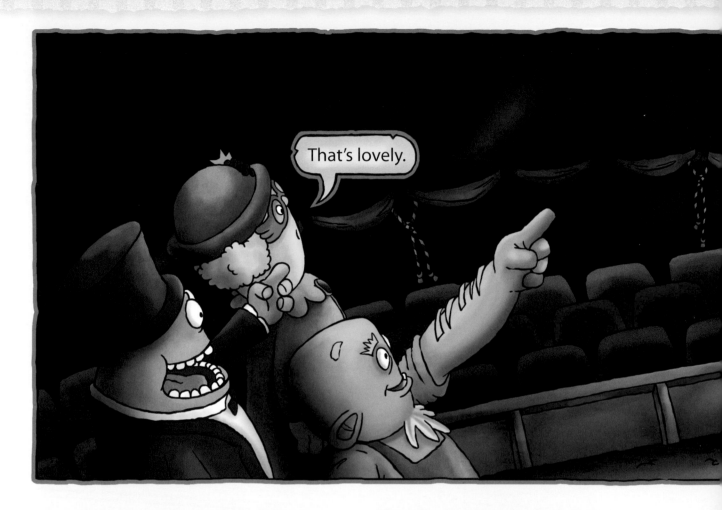

The Fabulous Fireflies are the last act. After the nasty shock of Monstro, everyone is a bit nervous when a large box appears in the ring. It makes a strange buzzing noise. A small flap in the top opens and out pour the Fireflies.

They make a shining golden cloud above the ring. Then they stream off in single file drawing a glowing circle of

light around the tent. As they flap their wings faster they glow more brightly.

They fly like acrobats tracing shapes in the air – circles and loops, lines and curves. Finally, they hover above the circus ring and slowly the word Goodnight appears. Everyone bursts into applause.

Guv turns to Mrs. Spectacles and says, 'I think we've just found our final act.'

Which acts would you choose for the circus?

As everybody is leaving, Mrs. Spectacles finds Monstro sitting outside the tent. He looks very sad.

'I'm sorry,' he says, 'I didn't mean to frighten you all. I just get carried away sometimes. But I really, really want to be in the circus.'

'Well, we can't scare people away. Is there anything else you can do?' Mrs. Spectacles asks.

'The only other thing I'm good at is cooking, but that's not much use in a circus.'

'You might be wrong there,' says Mrs. Spectacles. 'First, you must show me what you can do. But you must promise not to do anything horrible. Come back in the morning.'

The next day, Monstro and Mrs. Spectacles shut themselves away. Monstro turns out to be an amazing cook. He can make popcorn that glows in the dark, jellies that bounce up and down, ice cream that tastes of bacon and eggs.

'I love creating new foods,' he tells Mrs. Spectacles,' but most people just want the same things all the time.'

'This is just what the circus needs. You can be Monstro the Master Chef.' Mrs. Spectacles is really excited.

 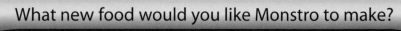 What new food would you like Monstro to make?

The next two weeks are madness as all the acts practise hard. There are new costumes to make and new music for The Cosmic Waves to rehearse. Gobi has to build props and make sure everything works. Monstro works hard on his recipes. Guv and Mrs. Spectacles rush round with posters and leaflets. Soon everyone has heard that the circus has some amazing new acts.

The opening night is sold out. Everything goes well. The people watching laugh at Mr. Scatterbrain. They cheer Lokankee and Magu. They love Tiny and Baked Bean. They gasp at the Fireflies.

Only Baked Bean is a bit unhappy. He still feels that a real dragon should be able to breathe fire as well as fly. But however hard he tries, he can only manage a little puff of smoke.

Outside the Big Top, Monstro is cooking up a storm. He has some amazing food on sale. The most popular is his ice cream. He has six new flavours – salt and vinegar, roast chicken, apple crumble, bubble gum, spicy curry, as well as the bacon and eggs one he made for Mrs. Spectacles.

People are surprised when they first try them, but then they come back for more. When he gets really busy, Monstro just grows a few more arms to help out. Everyone loves this too.

He is soon as famous as the circus and some people come just for his food. The circus crew also loves what he cooks. Baked Bean is very keen on the ice cream and licks out the bowls when he thinks no one is looking. Monstro is happy at last.

Mrs. Spectacles is delighted but also a bit worried. 'Just don't get carried away again, Monstro,' she warns him.

But one night Monstro does get carried away. He tries out more and more strange tastes for his ice cream. Some are good, some are not so good.

Tonight he is really busy and even with six arms he can't cope. He's trying to serve people and to mix up more ice cream at the same time. He is going too fast and tips a whole bottle of extra hot

chilli sauce into the ice cream by mistake. He doesn't notice because although he has six arms he still only has two eyes.

He mixes up the ice cream and gives a big cone to the next child. She licks it slowly. She doesn't know what flavour to expect.

Do you think this ice cream will taste good?

The little girl licks the ice cream again. At first it just tastes cold, then her mouth starts to feel warm. Then it gets hot. Then it feels as if it's on fire.

She drops the ice cream and bursts into tears. Mrs. Spectacles comes running up.

'Oh no! What's wrong?' she cries.

Baked Bean has been watching. He sees the little girl drop the ice cream. As Mrs. Spectacles leads her away, he sneaks up and licks it all up while no one is looking. He just can't get enough of Monstro's ice cream.

Baked Bean has just finished when he hears the music for the grand finale coming from the Big Top. He rushes into the circus ring.

  Do you think Baked Bean will like the ice cream?

Baked Bean opens his mouth to try and cool off. He breathes out really hard. But his breath is so hot that the glowing Fireflies set it alight. It turns into an amazing jet of fire.

The audience roars. They think it is all part of the show. Baked Bean looks surprised and then delighted. At last he has breathed fire.

Baked Bean is late and in the wrong place. He should be over by Tiny but he's standing just under the Fireflies.

He's also starting to feel very warm. It's not just his mouth that is hot but his whole body is on fire. Even the Fireflies can feel it and they flap even faster to cool him down.

Mrs. Spectacles realises what has happened. She is very pleased for Baked Bean but cross with Monstro.

'You can make some more chilli ice cream for Baked Bean, but you mustn't give it to anyone else. We don't want our audience bursting into flames.'

Baked Bean is just delighted that he can breathe fire and eat ice cream every night.